Everyday Wisdom

Everyday Wisdom

A Guide to a Better, Deeper Life

John C. Morgan

RESOURCE *Publications* · Eugene, Oregon

EVERYDAY WISDOM
A Guide to a Better, Deeper Life

Copyright © 2022 John C. Morgan. All rights reserved. Except for brief quotations in critical publications or reviews, no part of this book may be reproduced in any manner without prior written permission from the publisher. Write: Permissions, Wipf and Stock Publishers, 199 W. 8th Ave., Suite 3, Eugene, OR 97401.

Resource Publications
An Imprint of Wipf and Stock Publishers
199 W. 8th Ave., Suite 3
Eugene, OR 97401

www.wipfandstock.com

PAPERBACK ISBN: 978-1-6667-4854-3
HARDCOVER ISBN: 978-1-6667-4855-0
EBOOK ISBN: 978-1-6667-4856-7

01/03/23

Permission has been granted to use columns appearing in *The Mercury* newspaper and sister publications owned by MediaNews Group under the title "Everyday Ethics."

Permission has been granted to use columns appearing in the *Reading Eagle* under the title "Everyday Ethics."

"Garden" (here, "Tend a Garden") was first published in the May 2004 *Friends Journal* (www.friendsjournal.org) and is used with permission.

For my brother, Richard Lyon Morgan, friend and mentor

Contents

Preface | ix

1. Live Fully Every Day | 1
2. Think of Your Life as an Uncertain Journey | 3
3. "Know Yourself" | 7
4. Be Loving | 9
5. Live Peacefully | 11
6. Develop Your Character | 13
7. Learn to Listen | 15
8. Be Forgiving | 17
9. Become Like a Hedgehog | 20
10. Don't Be Fooled | 22
11. Practice Self-Reflection | 24
12. Grow Up | 26
13. Become a Pine Knotter | 28
14. Be Childlike | 30
15. Serve Others | 32
16. Nurture Your Soul | 34
17. Stifle Your Pride | 36
18. Stay Awake to the Day | 37
19. Take Care of Yourself | 39
20. Try Not to Lie (Too Often) | 41
21. Pay Attention to the Seasons | 43
22. Have a Heart | 45
23. Make Wise Decisions | 47
24. Practice Being Kind | 50

25. Turn Off, Tune In, Drop In | 52
26. Say and Act What You Believe | 54
27. Shape, Don't Fear, the Unknown | 56
28. Think before Acting | 58
29. Think of the Ends and Means | 60
30. Be a Hero | 62
31. Tend a Garden | 64
32. Use Common Sense | 66
33. Become a Role Model | 68
34. Assume the Middle Way | 70
35. Practice Dying | 72
36. Temporarily Suspend Doubt | 74
37. Don't Waste Time | 76
38. Find Your Story | 78
39. Stay Curious | 80
40. Ten Suggestions for Living Well | 82

Exercises for Self-Reflection | 85
   Create Your Book of Life | 85
   Keep a Journal | 86
   Conduct Your Annual Checkup | 88

About the Author | 91

Preface

I'VE TAUGHT AND WRITTEN about ethical issues for a long time. Sometimes the words felt stuffy with little impact on the lives of people who probably never have taken a philosophy course but still raised some of the same life questions philosophers addressed. My thoughts seemed to be a great gulf between the academic world and everyday life. It wasn't until I began to write a newspaper column, "Everyday Ethics," every week for years that I began to understand more fully and appreciate the importance of philosophy in the world outside the academy.

The selected essays here are from many columns I have written and shared with a much larger audience than I would have if I had limited them to classroom lectures. I believe they are modern-day ways to share philosophy with many outside of the academic classroom, just as some ancient philosophers took their teachings to the marketplace and some to schools of philosophy held outside in gardens.

There are three basic ways to express your thoughts about anything: Opinions, knowledge and wisdom.

Opinions are your personal reflections on any subject, from politics to sports. They may or may not be based on facts and can change over time, although some opinions get stuck and don't change, even when new evidence suggests they should.

I realize that sometimes there are so many conflicting opinions it's difficult to decide which one is correct. The only way I know to do so is to look for facts or evidence supporting one of

Preface

the opinions, the scientific method in other words. Opinions are meant to be updated even dropped over time. The person with the same opinion over a lifetime has either stumbled on a great, universal truth or failed to grow at all.

Knowledge is based not only on your own reflections but that of others. It generally is the accrued, reliable understandings of many others in other words. Knowledge changes over time, but not as rapidly as an opinion

Wisdom is about how best to live, whether as individuals or societies, based on the personal and collective experiences of many trusted resources. Wisdom takes a long time to grow and with regard to some basic truths, such as love your neighbor, may not change at all.

I usually write about things I think I know based on facts and interpretations of those facts, understanding that my knowledge is open to new understandings. In other words, I recognize that over time knowledge changes I also try to write about wisdom, knowledge I have gained for living or from other the world's great teachers.

This book is intended to be a practical guide to living a deeper, richer life in the everyday world. I hope it helps people reflect on their lives, to use some of the insights offered. I would suggest reading one short essay a day, in the morning or at bedtime, and taking the time to reflect on your own life. It's that simple to do but often easy to let slip. Practicing self-reflection every day is the key to a better life.

Here's a suggestion for how to use this book to help you live well. Read one path or guide a day, then pause and apply the wisdom to your own life. Make a few notes about what you learned in your journal or this book. Take time to do the exercises at the end of this book. If you are part of a small group or can create one, have each member complete the exercises, then share the findings.

John C. Morgan

1. Live Fully Every Day

EVERYDAY ETHICS IS THE clue to what really matters—how best to live fully each day.

We often forget this simple truth because our minds are diverted by wars and rumors of wars, floods and hurricanes, politics and other so-called big issues. But the bigger issues are usually in front of us, in the daily news of our lives.

I took time to think about what I learned about how best to live, day by day, and tried to be simple. Here's what I concluded and wrote down as a few basic rules to guide how I spend time.

Keep it simple; it will get complex all by itself. It's quite difficult to live simply so that others might simply live. Our lives are congested by things we think we need but really don't.

Fall back, spring ahead. Take time for self-care, the inner work of learning how to respect yourself.

Love more, hate less. Love is the glue which keeps our lives intact. Hate abuses not only others but oneself, wasting time in other words.

Focus energy on what can be changed, not what can't be changed. We spend too much time on what cannot be changed, living in the past rather than the present.

Treat others as you wish to be treated. It's the golden rule for how best to live.

In the ethic classes I taught, I suggested to students that their lives were the textbooks upon which their time would be spent. Each student was required to complete their own Book of Life, the principle being that self-reflection is one of the most important tasks they have. Or as Socrates said: "Know thyself."

The idea of completing a Book of Life was that each life is roughly composed of seven-year chapters. Each student was asked to jot down events or episodes for each seven-year chapter. Conveniently seven years translated into basic life chapters, one to seven being early childhood, eight to fifteen the growing up years, etc.

Then, in small groups, each student shared his or her life story. Others were asked to practice active listening. It shouldn't have surprised me, but did, how few students ever took the time to reflect on their own lives, much less listen to others. I think it is these small groups that everyday ethics happens.

So let me give you an assignment. Complete your Book of Life (a way to do so is at the back of this book). Mark off seven-year chapters, for example chapter one, birth to seven years old. Continue the chapters up to your current age.

Then sit down and look at your book of life. Reflect on it. Find another person or even a small group to share your stories. This is the heart of learning how best to live.

2. Think of Your Life as an Uncertain Journey

LET'S BE CLEAR: LIFE's journey can be confusing and requires a commitment to learning how to a live without many certainties, while at the same time learning to set boundaries to avoid freefall into the confusing abyss. One lifetime is not enough to explore more than a very few religious traditions, and even then, one sometimes sacrifices depth of understanding because there are so many layers of histories, personalities, and issues.

I grew up in a family with a long tradition of Christian preachers, but I admit the more I study the books and teachings of Christianity, the less I find myself really having knowledge, much less understanding. I spent years living within a Christian community and many decades studying the Bible or other writers within that tradition, and yet I find myself often bewildered by the confusing array of various denominations and movements all calling themselves Christian, and sometimes at odds with one another. Unless one throws up one's hands and says none of them are worth the effort, it is best to admit never feeling one has arrived. In fact, the image of the seeker or traveler is a good one to hold close, even as one wishes to find a home.

A few years ago, I decided to start a journal to record dreams I remembered from the night before. Each morning I wrote them down. I know I had many more dreams than I remembered when I woke up and even those which I did remember were only snippets from the entire dream, probably those in the last minutes of my sleep. Not that long ago I returned to my journal and read what I had written, and though not every dream made sense on its own when viewed as a whole, a theme did emerge, and it was mainly about being lost.

I will leave it to dream analysts to offer the deeper psychological meanings of my dreams—whether they were about emotions or triggers for something in my previous day that I was still working on—but I can report a common theme running through many years—the sense of feeling lost, usually in a large city and often trying to figure out how to get from a strange place to my home. Once I remember a dream in which my deceased sister was in a large, multi-room house trying to give me directions; another time I was hopelessly lost in a very large urban setting, going around in circles searching for a way out of the maze of back alleys.

But a dream this week took on a different quality at the end. I was still lost, this time trying to find a subway train to get somewhere or other. I was carrying a folder stuffed with papers; I am not even sure what was in that folder. But I got lost again, dropped the folder, and ended up in an underground station. I remember the feeling this time of knowing where I was, of relief and joyful I was home, not lost but found.

I believe the theme of being lost and then found is a great one, perhaps universal, a description of the human journey from anxiety and despair to ataraxia (the Stoic sense of being at one with oneself and the universe). I knew in a far deeper way than I had known before what the dream revealed: that I was found—by whom or what I am not sure. Perhaps the end of my journey through time will be discovering who and where I am.

Think about the parables of Jesus as examples of where this pattern of being lost and found emerges. There's the lost sheep as the most familiar, but also the lost coin and even the story of the prodigal son lost but then recovered. Each of these is about the experience of being found (in the vernacular of my ancestors, "saved"). But from what was I being saved? I felt I knew the answer: from myself, my feelings of being lost. And who saved me? That's one that like Jacob wrestling with an angel seeking a

2. Think of Your Life as an Uncertain Journey

blessing, I am still working on. I suppose I could say God saved me, but I wouldn't be honest with myself if I made that claim. All I can report is that after years of dreams about being lost, I was found. That's the essence of what the dream means to me. I was the prodigal returning home, welcomed with open arms.

As a child, I remember going with my mother to a big department store in downtown Philadelphia. We usually went near Christmas to see all the decorations and hear the organist playing carols. I got lost. But what I remember is my mother telling me beforehand that if I did get lost, I should go and stand under a statue of a giant eagle on the first floor. Her words led me there and though I was crying when she found me, she did find me. I can see the statue of the eagle even now, now looking like a brown angel with white tipped wings.

Since that dream, there have been some not-so-subtle changes in my life, inner and outer. I have felt a deeper sense of calm, an understanding that home is not a place but a new way of being in the world. Whether the external changes were always possible and I was the one not looking or if these external factors arose almost as a result of my inner reality, I don't know. The word synchronicity is one that feels true to my life recently. Synchronicity means a life event or happening that seems to take place as a meaningful coincidence. Something or someone has changed in my life. I am not questioning this, only trying to understand better what that means.

Lately, I have come to wonder if the deeper wisdom of most world spiritual traditions is that of being found after being lost. Buddha finds a way out of suffering. Jesus loses in the eyes of the world but gains in the eyes of all who follow him. Moses finds the Promised Land after being lost in the desert. Each one of us, especially myself, know what it means to feel lost so that when we find ourselves or are found, we find joy and peace. The wisdom for all religious mutts, then, is to understand the journey will contain losses and gains, that there may be no certain end, but that one may discover the incredible feeling of having been found and peacefulness.

Everyday Wisdom

Finally, I have neared the end of my travels and realized anew that home is not a resting place but a time of finding other sojourners on a journey one recognizes as almost the same as yours. Maybe this is what it's all been about.

3. "Know Yourself"

"Know yourself" was the guidance given both by the famous Oracle of Delphi in Greece and the philosopher Socrates. It's also the advice easy to give others and difficult to follow oneself.

I am the prime example of someone who gives advice to others and fails to follow it himself. I am prone to working too hard. I once saw this wise saying on a hospital chaplain's wall: Remember you are a human being, not a human doing.

Last week in an effort to review the final copy of what is now the book you now are reading, I raced through it and failed to note this chapter had been repeated exactly as shown here in a later one under a different title.

At first, I laughed at myself, then panicked realizing how embarrassing it would be to me when readers discovered the error. But the everyday wisdom about knowing yourself was driven home—I failed to follow my own guidance.

So, the wisdom I gained from everyday living was to stop rushing around and start taking time to be clear about what I was doing and relax. Rome was not built in a day but took time, patience and help.

I hope I learned a lesson: Slow down, if you feel rushed to finish something stall for time.

What can be postponed for tomorrow should be. It probably wasn't worth solving quickly in any case.

In retrospect what wisdom I gained about myself from the admonition to know yourself was twofold.

First, while sin has traditionally been defined as a transgression against some religious law, in more recent ways it has seen as an action that intentionally treats people as objects not subjects. It has often been seen as the putting yourself first, egoism in other words, often harming others.

For example, someone who puts himself first and measures success only in monetary terms may cause suffering to others willfully. This kind of behavior may be symbolized with images of darkness.

Second, there is also lightness within, the proclivity to act for others even when it might hurt oneself. The trick in living well is to seek light.

Moving from darkness to light in our lives means not letting the good fall victim to the perfect, but making small changes for the good piece by piece, even failing but still keeping watch over that which enhances life.

Light, which helps us see, even our own imperfections and judge others less harshly. We can move toward the light within ourselves and others when we see clearly, we are part of each other and this fragile planet circling a third—rate sun somewhere in a vast cosmos we cannot yet see its limits.

4. Be Loving

LOVE IS THE MOST important quality for a deeper and more fulfilling life.

Love has many dimensions, from destructive about a terrible relationship, to creative where people are committed not only to their own needs but those of others.

The older I get the more convinced I am that love is the most abused yet most important word in our lives. Some abuse love to get attention or power over someone, while others act lovingly to show affection to others in ways that help them.

The Greeks had four words that help to unlock the dimensions of love.

The first Greek word is eros, which is the emotional dimension of love. It's commonly used for what we mean by romantic love. It's powerful, sometimes carrying us to places where in retrospect we wish we'd never been. But, face it, without, not many of us would ever have arrived on this planet. But it usually cannot be sustained over the long haul. Love is more than a one-night stand.

Storge is another dimension of love which is essential the love of a parent for a child, or vice-versa. It is from the early forms of love in the family that our lives emerge for good or ill. Helping parents learn how best to raise a child is one of the most neglected learning experiences. We often are taught our parental skills by our parents and thus tend to repeat them in educating our own children.

Another word for love is philia, a deep relationship of friends over time. In the early days of philosophy in Greece, learners gathered in small groups to listen and learn from one another. The word "philosophy" comes about to mean the lovers of wisdom. It's often lacking in our modern culture where people seldom gather in small groups to learn from one another.

Agape is another form of love which is the rarest. It's the kind of love that acts to treat the other as kindly as one treats oneself. It is not egotistical or selfish but full of good intentions. It's a kind of love some theologians say is divine.

I have come to understand love as the most powerful force for good. While it involves our feelings, it is more. Love is more an act which requires commitment. Nothing sustains and helps us more than loving and being loved.

5. Live Peacefully

WE LIVE IN TIMES of ethical turmoil, divisions between those who believe only their truths are true and others who believe there are no universal truths at all. When these two points of view clash there is confusion, conflict and often breakdowns of social norms that bind us together.

Those who believe only their truths are real often try to suppress those who don't believe the same. Those who believe there are no universal truths sow confusion when the cultural fabric tears into competing values.

Is there any way to live in peace?

An eighteenth-century philosopher, Immanuel Kant, said there was.

Kant believed no human being has all the truth. The starry heavens above were deeper than the ability of human beings to grasp any final truths. But he also believed in a moral law within every person that could be understood and lived. He called this law the categorical imperative.

The categorical imperative is the most fundamental and best way to live fully, as individuals and a whole society. It is a reliable guide to ethical behavior.

What is the categorical imperative?

Kant wrote there were two main parts of the categorical imperative. The first would be to so act that if your actions were realized, they would be good for everyone. I often see this as a *what if* question. Expressed negatively one might ask: What if everyone lied? Or, in a positive way, what if people treated one another kindly, what kind of society would that mean? Or, apply the principle to oneself: What if I cheated on a test or my tax returns or my spouse, would any of these be good ways for people to behave?

The second part of Kant's categorical imperative is: Treat people as ends unto themselves and not as means to something else. Simply put, treat people as subjects worthy of respect and not as objects manipulated for some other reason.

I sometimes wonder what kind of world it might be if we really lived the two basic principles of Immanuel Kant, not only in our personal lives but in our society.

Would we stop putting labels on people because of their age or sex or gender or nationality and see in every human being a thou and not an it?

Would we pause before acting and ask ourselves as individuals and nations what might be the results of our actions on others?

The best example of Kant's philosophy is the Golden Rule: Treat others as you wish to be treated. I have found various versions of this rule in fourteen world traditions, and I suspect there are other mentions of the rule I have not discovered.

The test of the Golden Rule is putting it into action, treating others as we wish to be treated.

6. Develop Your Character

Character matters.

You find out about character when you encounter someone who doesn't have it but lies, cheats, and hurts others. It's the negative characters who get our attention.

But there are also positive characters, ones who inspire us to be better people ourselves. We don't notice them as often because they go about their lives not asking to be praised or noticed. Their strength comes from within.

But what is character?

Character is who you are when no one is looking. It is the combination of your genes, choices, and behavior over a lifetime that show who you really are, not who others think you are or even who you think you are.

Here's the basic thought about character: Who you are in the deepest part of yourself shapes what happens to yourself and others.

You can't blame your genes or your upbringing completely for the choices you have made, although you can often be shaped by the circumstances in which you find yourself, especially when growing up. But I have often found the people I most admire are those who have come from difficult beginnings but by their own choices and hard work become better human beings.

But you become a better person by practicing who you want to be. Practice may not make you perfect, but it does make you a better person if you try to live by the what you say you believe.

What really harms oneself and others is professing to believe something then acting otherwise.

If you want to be a compassionate person, practice being kind. The same applies if you want to be a thoughtful person—practice being thoughtful.

I know it is not politically correct these days to speak about role models, but I think role models are important, both for individual and societal well-being. And they are not always the obvious choices.

One of my role models was Bill, the janitor where I went to school. He simply hung around the cafeteria and listened. He had no formal degree except that of learning from life itself. But he practiced compassion, the gift of listening to someone without judging them, helping them reach their own decisions. When I taught, he was the example I tried to follow.

I once asked Bill what motivated him to act this way, and he responded: "I just try to treat others as I want to be treated." That's character.

I think about the character of Bill in the light of some of the political figures of our time who cheat, steal and lie their way to power and fame. What kind of role models are they for others, especially children?

Of course, there are ethical politicians just as there are moral people in every vocation. The one I consult often for his wisdom is Marcus Aurelius, the Roman emperor who came to power in 161 A.D. during a time of wars and internal problems. This morning, I was reading his Meditations, and his words about being a wise and compassionate person reached out across the centuries to remind me that even people in power can display great character

Perhaps if our political, religious, and civic leaders told the truth, practiced compassion, and sought justice, we'd have better role models and society.

7. Learn to Listen

ONE THING A WRITER needs to survive is a thick skin.

One thing a writer needs to thrive is the ability to listen.

If you are a reporter or editor you learn to deal with critics. You understand that it is often the ones with the biggest gripes who respond most often. Once you realize this, you take the readers who respond with praise more thankfully. But you listen to both in the hope of learning something about yourself.

Recently after a column about democracy, I was called a "liberal," then a "conservative." The labels were hurled at me more as weapons than a means of communication.

I accept both definitions if the original meanings of the words are used. Liberal in its Latin origins means "free." I affirm freedom as a necessary quality for living in a democracy. In older usage, liberal means "generous," and I try to treat others as kindly as I would wish to be treated myself.

As to being a conservative, I do believe there are many values from the past that need to be brought into the present. One of the values I most cherish is that of character, that quality of a human being that seeks to live the values of truthfulness and compassion.

But tossing labels at someone without understanding what they mean is the mark of small minds and closed hearts. Labels are intended to be put on products, not people. People are more complicated than a single tag.

The use of labels is another mark of the lack of what is called "civil discourse" in our society, the ability to present one's own opinions while being willing to listen to another's point of view no matter how different from one's own. Listening is a rare skill these days in a world clogged with meaningless words.

These days we seem to argue not listen, to seek to prove a point not to engage in dialog.

Are there constructive ways to communicate when values clash?

Because as a writer and speaker, words are the tools of my trade, I have learned a few simple lessons I keep handy to remind myself of how best to communicate.

1. Speak your truth in love.

2. Keep it simple; it will get complex all by itself.

3. Don't take criticism personally. Ask yourself if the critic's words can improve what you say or write.

8. Be Forgiving

I KNEW WHAT I was doing was wrong starting a fire in the garage outside the house where we lived. To make it worse, we didn't even own the garage or the house to which it belonged. It was part of the package for being the minister of the church my father served and I was intentionally hoping to burn it down.

I wish I could claim I was a mere child playing with matches, but that would be a lie and, as every preacher's kid knows, it was hell growing up in a parsonage where like every one of your words or deeds were under the bright lights of an unforgiving church membership. Now I realize my act was deliberate, showing my disdain for the people my father served, knowing that from a distance they seemed fine folks but up close swore, smoked, engaged in bitter criticisms, and criticized your father for their shortcomings.

Hell, I wanted them all to burn in that inferno reserved for unbelievers like myself, who at the age of seven thought I didn't believe in God but did enjoy the stories of Jesus, especially the ones about lost sheep and the prodigal son. I understood the meaning of these stories from personal experience, even at seven years old. I felt lost and abandoned as the youngest of five, finding out that I was a mistake, an unintended consequence of the dying flame of my parents' marriage. It took me years to turn this supposed problem into a strength. After all, I wasn't meant to be here, so anything I did was better than nothing.

It wasn't just a rebellion against the church that led me to start lighting a match to burn the garage down. It was more personal than that, a strike against hypocrisy. You see my older brother had cages in the garage in which he helped wounded pigeons heal. Praise was heaped on him for his acts of Christian mercy. What they didn't know I did because I watched him shoot pigeons perched on the roof with his high-powered sling shot, then put them in cages. He symbolized the very hypocrisy I saw in church life—people talking about loving neighbors then acting out their aggressions against others, principally the African American neighbors on Spruce Street, the ones who cleaned their houses and the church building and took care of their children.

I felt a strange feeling of delight as I prepared to light a crumpled-up newspaper with matches taken from my father's study. Not even the cooing of pigeons or the fear of going to hell I'd heard preached stopped me. This would be the ultimate payback.

As I struck the match and lit a corner of the newspaper and smoke began to swirl, I heard a voice behind me. "Johnny, what are you doing?" My sister had been in our backyard and wondered why the garage door was open. She raced in, stomped out the small fire, and grabbed me. "You could have burnt the garage down, not to say killed your brother's pigeons." She took my hand and said she was taking me to my father's third floor study where I could explain to him what I was doing. I remember bursting into tears and trying to resist being pulled up the three flights of stars. The fear of what my father might do to me was terrifying. I feared he would beat the hell out of me.

My father's desk was quite large, his father's and brought across the ocean from London. As a child it seemed gigantic. As we entered his room, I could barely see his head above the top of the desk. When he stood up, I felt as if God were there ready to confirm a judgment. When my sister told him what I had been doing, I expected to be sent to my room to languish there for at least the day. He stared at me, and said: "Don't do it again." He then sat down in his chair and continued working. My sister led me out of the room saying quietly: "You got off lightly this time."

I felt relieved, my expectations of being punished gone. If a father represents God to young children, I changed my

8. Be Forgiving

understanding of who the prime mover of the cosmos must be like, more forgiving than I had thought, more like a mother than father. In such seemingly small episodes in our lives, often when we are children, the child remains in us as we grow older. Luckily for me, the universe might still have rough edges, but they are not so terrifying.

I never thanked my father for being benevolent, but I am not sure his Calvinistic heart would have welcomed my gratitude But I am grateful nonetheless for having been caught in the act of burning down the garage. It saved me from going to hell.

9. Become Like a Hedgehog

HERE'S SOME ADVICE FROM a hedgehog, told in an ancient Greek story, most of it lost in time-but the essential part remains. Stories unlock wisdom, which is why they are so often repeated. In case you have never seen a hedgehog, often found along roads in England, the creature is small, usually brown, quite cute from a distance.

The conclusion of the story about the fox and the hedgehog is that while foxes supposedly know many things, the hedgehog's one piece of knowledge is the best of all—it has to do with staying alive, and that's pretty essential.

You see, when threatened, the hedgehog is able to roll up into a small ball and protect himself by raising the prickly needles on his outer layer. While the fox may run in many directions to avoid danger, the hedgehog stands his ground and does one thing well, a good word of advice for us today who are tossed and turned in many directions without actually getting anywhere.

The groundhog may be a star in Pennsylvania folklore, but in the British Isles where hedgehogs are plentiful, he is a reminder of one of life's great pieces of wisdom—sometimes it is better to know a lot about a great thing than a great deal about things not so important.

Many political leaders are by and large foxes who think they know a lot but really don't, even while pretending they do. But in our time, hedgehog thinkers are rare because most of our minds are cluttered with verbal garbage, unless, of course, from time to

9. Become Like a Hedgehog

time we pause to actually reflect on the words of a great poem or even our own lives.

Don't misunderstand. The hedgehog philosophy can also hold onto one big lie and call it a "truth" such as some such as some races or religious or political philosophies are true while all the rest false.

One truth I've learned over the years is this one: Learn what can be changed from what can't.

One can apply this to any life situation with which you are faced, especially one that may be troublesome. You may not be able to get out of the situation immediately, but you always have the ultimate freedom to choose your attitude. I know some whose attitudes make situations worse, and others whose attitudes end up changing not only their inner lives but also the situation itself. By choosing how you respond to any situation, you exercise power over it.

Attitudes may not change the situation in which you find yourself; but they do change you, and perhaps that is the best wisdom of all a poor little hedgehog can offer.

10. Don't Be Fooled

"Fool me once, shame on you. Fool me twice, shame on me."

This is an old saying from nearly four centuries ago which is a reminder about not being fooled a second time by the same person.

There are many dangers telling lies. The liar eventually can't be trusted to tell the truth, which leads having to tell more lies to cover up the first one. The old fable of the boy who cried wolf too often and then a real wolf appeared, and no one believed him.

There are times I wonder if the liar realizes she or he is lying. The problem these days is that we are so inundated with half-truths and outright lies it is difficult to decide what is an outright lie or exaggeration or truthful.

But that old aphorism about being fooled once and then twice got me thinking about a different understanding of those words. The obvious interpretation is that if you are fooled twice by the same speaker, the problem is yours. Liars don't stop telling lies until they are called out, and sometimes not even then when they lie more to cover up the first lie and need to be called out a few more times.

Ethics is sometimes called the "practical philosophy" because it deals with real life issues. That's why I use a lot of case studies in the classes I teach as a way of assessing life situations. Of course, names are changed to protect identities, but the situations are real. Each student then presents his or her case study in a small group which provides insights.

10. Don't Be Fooled

There is one case I remember from a student, call her Ruth. She had been in a long-term relationship with another student and they were thinking about getting married after graduation. She heard from a friend that he was cheating on her. She confronted him and he confessed, promising not to repeat the same mistake. He did and again she confronted him with the same result—he cheated again. She believed everyone deserved a second change, so she forgave him again—and he was caught a third time. This time she broke off the relationship.

The conclusion to her case study was this. "I realized I was not strong enough to call him out. The problem was with me allowing myself to be fooled. I vowed not to be fooled again."

Liars will continue their lies if not confronted by those being lied to.

11. Practice Self-Reflection

When he was asked what was the most important guidance he could offer, the philosopher Socrates responded that knowing yourself was among the wisest. It's called self-reflection, an exercise many do not pursue because they don't think about it or believe they don't have the time.

Self-reflection is a choice which requires a commitment. Some adopt a daily practice of taking a few minutes every day to reflect on their lives. The purpose of taking time is to look at what can and cannot be changed. Ethics, after all, is a practical philosophy intended to improve the quality of one's life.

The same process also applies to whole societies and is called social ethics. This requires a nation from time to time to take stock of what it is doing and where it might be headed. Without knowing its strengths and weaknesses and adapting to changes, stagnation and frustration result.

Not reflecting on personal or societal statuses but plunging ahead without thought reminds me of the story of a ship at sea during a great storm. Worried passengers approached the captain to express their concerns. "Don't worry," responded the captain, "I'm not sure where we are, but we're getting there twice as fast."

The word "philosophy" means the love of wisdom and implies learning how best to live. We are a species with the ability to think for ourselves, though it may be difficult to accept when we let ourselves be duped by lies.

11. Practice Self-Reflection

Wisdom is the practice of self-reflection, of thinking on decisions before jumping in, of seeking to understand our intentions and those of others, of seeking truth as best we can. In the animal world, stimulus and response are the basic means of behavior. While we belong to the animal realm, we also are equipped with the ability to think critically using our reason,

I have found a question that helps me to reflect on my life and can be applied to most situations: What if?

For example, in looking at your choice of vocation, you might ask yourself: What if I had not become a teacher? What else might have become? You might have concluded you might have become a writer.

Of, what if I had not moved to another place, how might my life have changed?

Answering what-if questions can result either in decisions you are proud of or ones you regret. In either case, you learn something about the twists in your life and mistakes you have made sometimes offer clues about what not to do the next time.

The purpose of self-reflection is not to adopt a woe-is-me attitude, but rather to look honestly at your life patterns, both the ones that have ended with regrets and others with a sense of accomplishment. You don't have to repeat decisions that left you confused or full of regrets, but you can seek to follow those behaviors which have led to happiness or fulfillment.

Maybe you can't change the past, but you can change the present. And that's why Socrates was right about knowing yourself. It's the source of power for yourself. Give up that power and you give up the greatest human gift: the ability to reason. And reflection on one's society is critical to making decisions that impact the present and future.

12. Grow Up

YOU LEARN A GREAT deal about how to live by watching children, especially when it comes to their conflicts.

Listen to some of what they say to understand how not to fight fairly.

"Did not! Did so! Did not! Did so!" (And the taunts continue for some time).

"Yeah, make me! No, you make me!" (And the taunts continue for some time).

"Step over this line. I dare you!" "No, you step over my line and see what happens." (No one steps over any line and nothing happens).

"Your mother is" (supply another derogatory description). "Says who? Your mother is_____." (Supply a harsher derogatory description).

And so, the conflict continues, often escalates, until someone, usually a teacher, intervenes. He or she usually asks what the struggle is about, which can end with more accusations hurled. "He called my mother a bad word," says one child. "You called my mother a bad word first," says the second child. "Did not," says the first. "Did so," responds the second.

Hopefully the teacher calms the children down and is wise enough to see the conflict as a learning lesson. She forces them to shake hands which, of course, does not deal with the conflict but only a temporary solution to avoid later bloodshed.

12. Grow Up

As you might imagine, this kind of conflict among children continues into adulthood, especially in the political realm where opposing party members hurl the most hurtful and often false verbal jabs at one another. Unlike children, some adult politicians use these jabs in their campaign ads to raise more money to stay in office or run for one. Unfortunately, their conflicts are fed by media commentators who compete with other media commentators to raise their rankings. Worse, there are literally millions of people online who already have formed opinions about any conflict and are happy to share their ignorance with as many others as possible, and they with still more.

I am not sure there is any easy answer to easing conflicts when few are interested in reaching consensus or even lessening the struggle. Sowing confusing and inflicting pain on others seems the real goal, not solving problems.

What might help would be suggesting, even requiring, anyone who runs for office to take a basic course in civic discourse, learning how to communicate fairly, looking for commonsense solutions, understanding compromise is not a bad word but one that describes the political process in democracies.

Here are two words from the school of common sense that could help find common ground: Discussion and dialogue. Discussion is like a tennis match where opponents hit the verbal tennis ball back and forth until someone winds. Dialogue is more like an exercise where common ground is the goal, neither opponent winning or losing, but each winning something other than vanquishing the opposition.

Discussion, from the Latin root which also forms concussion and percussion. Dialog, from the Latin root, to seek the meaning between. If we really focused on dialogue, we might actually find common ground and common-sense solutions. But that will require us to listen without judging and learn from one another.

Don't hold your breath waiting for dialog to happen. Or, perhaps, send any warring parties to the back of the room and make them sit there until they can act decently. Better, if all else fails, send them to a detention room where they must sit.

13. Become a Pine Knotter

PINE KNOTTERS UNITE! YOU have nothing to lose but your anxieties, and everything to gain.

For those of you who cut wood, you know what a pine knot is because you have a hard time sawing through it. It is the toughest part. I've tried to saw through a pine knot and after much cursing, gave up and cut around it.

Dead branches drop off healthy trees and wood knots appear where they died. Knots are the imperfections that cause living wood grain to grow around them.

So why am I writing about pine knots in wood?

Well, first because I moved here from a small town on the banks of the Susquehanna River, one envisioned as a refuge for those seeking freedom to believe and think as they wished. Its most famous early settler was Dr. Joseph Priestley, the "discover of oxygen" (as if anyone could discover something we use all the time), considered the parent of American chemistry. For his free thinking, Priestley's home in England had been burnt down by a mob.

It's almost a place where every year they celebrate Pine knotter Day with games and food in the center of an idyllic town, with a band shell and many trees lined the street. Walking there, I could well imagine running into Dr. Priestley himself, it was such a quaint place.

I find much in nature from which to learn. Sometimes the best teachers are those who ask us to stop, look, and listen to the

13. Become a Pine Knotter

world around us, especially the natural world. One can learn as much if not more from a river than a textbook. I have understood more from tending a garden than attending a class.

Indeed, the first words of many wisdom teachers is: "Wake up!" They ask us to witness the miracle of life in and around us, to spend a moment acknowledging its beauty and brevity.

So, what have I learned from pine knots?

First, they are tough. And their toughness comes from their imperfections. Strength comes from weakness, in other words. And that is an important lesson for living. Rather than denying our imperfections, we should learn and grow from them.

Second, pine knots are dead wood before being renewed. They are literally dead wood around which has grown living wood. Out of death, comes new life. That's another thought coming from many world wisdom traditions. Out of what appears to be loss, comes new life.

Think of a time in your life when you thought you had lost something or someone and how difficult that felt at the time. Then, reflect on what came out of that loss, a new beginning. I know I have learned more from any losses than gains.

The next time you feel weak, remember the noble pine knot, life out of death, strength out of weakness and imperfection.

14. Be Childlike

WORDS, LIKE TRUTH, MATTER.
Consider these two words: childlike and childish. Here are the dictionary definitions (from Merriam-Webster):
Childish: marked by suggestive immaturity and lack of poise. A childish spiteful remark.
Childlike: resembling, suggesting, or appropriate to a child, marked by innocence, trust, and ingenuousness. Childlike delight.

When I survey the scene these days it feels like a playground where childish rules are paramount and bullies reign while the childlike try to stay out of sight and wait for recess to end. It's not a fun place to be for the childlike. And a great place to be for the childish who don't play fair but fight at the drop of a hat. I don't remember much from what I learned in my elementary school classes, but I do remember the unchecked playground bullies who got their ways by taunting and yelling at others, especially the vulnerable.

All organizations have childlike and childish people. Where there are childlike leaders, the organization is healthy; where the childish reign, there is chaos. They call people names. They yell at others and seem incapable of listening to others. And when caught in negative behavior, they lie. They probably need a timeout and sent to a separate corner to think about their behaviors, but they lack the ability to reflect upon their own behaviors, usually blaming everyone else for their own shortcomings.

14. Be Childlike

Luckily, we have a few other political leaders who are more childlike. They trust themselves enough to listen to others, knowing they are sometimes wrong. They don't take everything as a personal attack, but seek dialog. They don't yell at others but listen. They speak softly. They are not bullies. They seek the common good, not just serve their own interests. They can reflect on their own behaviors, sometimes judging themselves more critically than others. They delight in the truth.

I'm sure you know childlike and childish persons wherever you live or work. They appear in most organizations. The trick is spotting them and not letting yourself be drawn into the drama of the childish (that feeds their already enlarged egos) and identifying the childlike and learning from them. If the childlike are in leadership positions, the organization they lead is healthy; if the childish lead, the organization is in chaos with factions fighting and nothing done.

What does it all mean for us?

Here are a few simple principles we should have learned in elementary school:

Trust how people act not what they say. Look for the childlike not childish leader who trusts himself and others to work toward common goals.

Don't fall for half-truths or fake news. Trust your own eyes, ears, and brain to know the difference between truths and lies. Watch what they do, not just what they spin.

Don't become childish yourself, thinking others are wrong and you are always right. Do not yell at those with a different opinion, but listen.

Think win/win. You are not out to vanquish what you think are opponents, but to grow. The mark of an immature person is always needing to win. It shows they don't trust themselves.

And finally, in dealing with a childish person, even yourself, follow the principle you should have learned in first grade: Go to the corner and sit quietly by yourself or ask the other person to do so for a few minutes until you or they are ready to play fair and not fight.

15. Serve Others

THE ANCIENT WISDOM TEACHERS knew well that learning how best to live could be summarized in a simple rule: Stop, look, and listen.

Stop being busy long enough to reflect on life. Look at what's around you. And listen to your own heart.

Stop, look and listen is a rule not only to be memorized but practiced every day until it becomes a way of life.

Yesterday as I went outside, I heard the honking of geese overhead and looked up to watch them flying in a V formation heading south.

Some years ago, while I was directing an organization, I observed a flock overhead and got to thinking why they flew in such a formation. Little did I realize until I read and thought more, that the geese offered me much guidance about leadership.

Geese fly in V formation because it enables them to fly greater distances by conserving their energy, thus reducing wind resistance. One bird flies in front, only falling back when tired and is then replaced by another. And when they honk, they are sending messages of support to the leader.

I compared this pattern of leadership to that which often rules today. Leaders who move out front and only want to be praised, who care for others only for what they can offer, who honk to criticize but not to support the team.

I learned about a different model called servant leadership, described by Robert Greenleaf, a corporate executive who for

15. Serve Others

more than 30 years worked at AT&T before retiring to teach and write.

Greenleaf's essay "The Servant as Leader" was published in 1970. In it, he argued the best leaders were servants first, not leading by telling others what to do or bullying them, but seeking to serve them. The best leaders embodied listening and persuasion skills. They led as much by who they were as what they told others to do.

That simple act of stopping long enough to look and listen to the geese overhead offered me more insight than I received from most of the management training courses I had taken.

I also learned that the same lesson applied to my life. I needed to stop from time to time to consider who and where I was, to take stock of things. It was the first lesson of philosophy: Know thyself.

I also grew to understand that sometimes all one need do is be aware of yourself and your surroundings It's another early philosophical lesson: Wake up!

And finally, I learned to listen to myself, the inner voice which tends to be drowned out in the clutter and confusion of life.

Stop, look, and listen. It's the beginning of learning how to live deeply.

16. Nurture Your Soul

But what's a soul?

It's the kind of question a child asks that stumps parents. It's akin to asking other great questions that children raise and adults try to answer such as asking what happens to someone after they die or what was there before there was nothing.

It may be that asking the questions is important even if the answers are difficult to answer. The philosopher Aristotle said that philosophy begins in wonder, so perhaps retaining a sense of wonder if the heart of what it means to be fully human.

I once asked students in a philosophy class whether they had souls and most looked at me with a puzzled, blank look on their faces. As we discussed the question, students said they had often wondered about the question but no one had ever asked them to answer it.

We had been talking about some of the early philosophers' thoughts about the soul, many simply saying the soul was spiritual to show its difference from the body or material. The soul was conceived as the immaterial part of the human being and, indeed, of all creatures.

The word "soul" is nephesh in Greek and refers to the inner self of each person—the mind, will, and emotions. When Jesus warned about losing one's soul in pursuit of other physical benefits such as accumulating wealth, it was this notion of the soul as the authentic self or real person.

16. Nurture Your Soul

Long ago the care of the soul was essential to wellbeing. Both Plato and Socrates believed that this effort was the most essential need of human beings. Socrates believed that the practice of doing philosophy—questioning and seeking truth—was taking care of our souls, a kind of therapy to promote healing and wholeness.

Of course, in some other traditions, the soul is the animating spirit of the whole cosmos, including plants and animals. Our dog and cats seem to have more soulfulness than some people I've known, and even trees feel full of an animating spirit.

It is also been written by historians that a nation can have a "soul," a network of animating principles, in our case the U.S. Constitution and Bill of Rights. It's why it hurts when people violate these basic norms by their actions—they are damaging our collective soul.

I suppose that one can spend a lifetime trying to define what soul is. It's the same kind of effort that some criticize for focusing on questions without clear answers, such as debating how many angels there are on the head of a pin.

But taking care of one's soul or inner spirit is just as important as taking care of one's body. A regular practice of taking time to reflect on one's life, living ethically, and honoring the soul within and without is essential.

It may never be possible to find a definition of the soul that is intellectually satisfying to everyone, but that misses the point. As an essential animating principle of life, the soul cannot be reduced to a simple formula. Perhaps that's why one of my students came up with the wisest response: "I can't define what the soul is, but I know it when I feel it."

17. Stifle Your Pride

WE DON'T REALLY KNOW much when it comes to measuring what we think we know against what is possible to know.

Humility is one of the great virtues because it shows the wisdom which understands the limits of our knowledge but also the openness to finding new ways of thinking—progress, in words.

Not all that long ago people believed Earth was the center of the universe. It took a telescope and Galileo looking through it to see that we were actually circling around the sun with other planets. Some resisted this new understanding because they realized it would changetheir understanding of the importance of human beings and their place in the universe. It required humility to make the transition to a new understanding.

The opposite of humility is pride, thinking oneself wiser and better than others, putting oneself at the center of the universe. In some traditions, pride is the source of evil. The Book of Proverbs, for example, notes that "when pride comes, then comes disgrace, but with the humble is wisdom" (Proverbs 11:2).

These are humble words, kept simple and short to get your attention. A long and scholarly article about humility seems prideful.

18. Stay Awake to the Day

You can remember the past but not really live in it. It resides in memories, perhaps many tainted or misplaced.

You can reflect on the future and even make plans for it, but you can't jump into it today. It dwells somewhere in hopes and fears, neither of which may be realized.

All you really have is now, and even that will pass before you realize it unless you are awake to the present.

Staying awake now is the guidance offered from many wisdom traditions over many ages. But it takes conscious awareness of the time in which you exist to follow this guidance.

Everything conspires to lure you away from awareness, to direct your attention from what some mystics call the Eternal Now, the one place that is most important—where past, present, and future may merge.

It seems to me that you have a choice of how best to live. You can choose to accept what others try to make you see, a kind of perpetual show-and-tell that leads you further away from yourself and closer to what someone else wants you to believe for their sake, not yours. Or you can choose to make the decision for yourself, practicing being aware of the inner and outer life that is today's gift.

It's not easy staying awake to life's daily gifts. You must stay awake every day by adopting some practice to help you. People adopt different practices to help themselves.

Everyday Wisdom

I take a few minutes every morning to read a short passage from wisdom teachers, but I spend most of the time being quiet and, strange as it might seem, letting go of any thoughts that invade my mind. It takes time to stop thinking, your mind cluttered with sounds and sights stored there.

Out of my life, I have found that what I pay attention to is often how I end up feeling. If I choose to focus on the worst, I probably end feeling bad, while the opposite also takes place.

Today I chose to welcome the morning by observing it breaking in front of me.

Here's my list of observations:

- The sun rising over a much cooler morning.
- Sparrows gathering seed on the ground.
- The sounds of leaves waving in the breeze.
- A neighbor getting up to go to work.
- The laughter of children going to school.
- A patchwork quilt of clouds.
- A black cat.
- Dogs barking.

In other words, I am awake.

19. Take Care of Yourself

A WISE TEACHER ONCE advised "take care of yourself, because no one will do that for you."

At the time that advise seemed downright selfish, putting yourself first above all else a recipe for behavior in which no one else counted except yourself. We are, after all, social animals living in a web of relationships, whether with people or nature.

It took me time to realize what the teacher meant. Only you have the power to practice self-love, which meant taking care of your body, mind, and spirit. If you don't take care of yourself, someone else will and their motivations might not be in your interest.

Self-care is not the same as selfishness. It's sometimes difficult to understand this if you have been taught to put others ahead of your own needs, an issue that impacts those in the helping professions most. For those who do so, usually putting the needs of others ahead of their own can lead to burnout and a lesser sense of self-worth may result.

Many wisdom traditions teach this basic truth: Treat others as kindly as you would treat yourself. Of, as Jesus said was the second great commandment: "Love your neighbor as yourself." Note, he did not say just love yourself or just love your neighbor. He connected self-love with love of neighbor.

I once knew a kind man who practiced this ethic of love of self with love of neighbor. He was a journalist with whom I worked side by side in my first job as a newspaper editor and reporter.

Being an African American who grew up in the days when this made life difficult, even painful. When he once was refused a haircut because of the color of his skin, he staged a boycott of the barbershop, day after day joined by others until the shop owner gave up and opened his service to everyone.

I once heard Dr. Martin Luther King Jr. give a speech in which he talked about the power of love to change hearts and minds. He preached non-violent love like Gandhi which sought to free both the one oppressed and the oppressor. It's tough love not what Dr. King called "emotional bosh."

What is "tough love"? It's being truthful, not letting yourself or the other person off the hook, thinking your being kind by doing so. You're not. By not being truthful, you're actually permitting the other person to continue their negative behavior and worse implicating yourself. A relationship based on lies is doomed to more suffering.

20. Try Not to Lie (Too Often)

THERE ARE MANY BIG lies these days that multiply like mosquitoes on a muggy summer night. Someone starts a big lie and it multiplies so fast on so many media outlets that it's nearly impossible to discover its origins or decide if it has any truth in it.

In our times big lies, if big enough and repeated often, grow without much ability to check them, in spite of fact-checkers. It seems the bigger the lie, the harder it is to stop its spread, so that sometimes a whole culture is immersed and truth is the loser.

Let's face it, while most of us don't have the platforms to spread big lies, we do find the need to use little, white lies many times. When we are confronted with our own little, white lies it's easier to deny we ever told a lie or that our small lies were intended to save someone's feelings.

Little, white lies are the stuff of which everyday life is made. We hide behind them to save others and ourselves the burden of whatever truth we don't want to face about ourselves.

As to the third ingredient of lies—statistics—we know that in the public media one person's statistics are another person's lies. Right now, as you read these words, I know that at least 75% of you agree with everything I am writing. (Well, it's just a little, white lie I am using to shade the truth).

When it comes to lies and truths, there are two conclusions I have come to see as important.

First, everyone lies, some more often than others. The difference is that some people don't realize they lie, while others use lies to hide the truth. Those who use lies intentionally are worse because they know they are lying to hide the truth or benefit themselves. This may explain why in many world spiritual traditions, Satan is seen as the great liar or deceiver.

Second, we live in dangerous times when facts don't seem to matter and falsehoods take on the mantle of truth. In such cases, truth dies the slow death of confusion, consternation and eventually its demise.

The best advice I can offer is to accept no statement as true unless you have examined it carefully, listened to facts that seem to be contrary, and then concluded tentatively what may be true. Note, the word "tentatively." Few truths survive the tests of time and critical inquiry, but when they do, pay attention. They are very important breakthroughs in times of twisted logic and lies.

21. Pay Attention to the Seasons

I SPENT THE WINTER grumbling and complaining about the cold and snow and threatening to move to a warmer climate. And then spring burst on the scene, a few warmer days when I could sit outside in the sun, hear the birds singing and see the emerging yellow daffodils.

The truth is I need the winter to rejoice in the renewal signs of April, just as I need summer to slow down, and the fall to prepare for the cold winter to come. The four seasons are ways we mark the passage of time. I would be bored if the only season were summer or even spring.

We can learn a great deal about how to live by paying attention to the seasons of our lives. Sometimes if we pay close attention, we can discover a deeper dimension of our everyday lives. Out of the supposed dying signs of winter arises new life.

One recent morning I spent a few minutes remembering a trip my two brothers and I made to England and Wales. We were attempting to discover the places where our ancestors lived.

We spent a few days in an inn across the street from the Tintern Abbey in Wales. It was a bright summer morning when I set out before the others arose to climb the hillside above the old abbey. I wanted to see the abbey from a higher point, which the monks who once called it the devil's pulpit because they felt Satan was trying to lure them away from their vows.

Once at the top of the hill I sat down under an old tree, its branches offering shelter. I don't know how long I rested there, but

I slowly became aware of what seemed a different time and dimension breaking into my consciousness. I later wrote a poem about that experience, little realizing until later that was on the same trail the English poet Wordsworth had traveled and later written one of his more famous poems, "Lines Composed a Few Miles above Tintern Abbey."

As I walked down the hill, I had a feeling that time as I understood it, measured by clocks, even passing seasons, had faded from my consciousness, and in its place a new awareness of a fuller, deeper dimension had arisen. Coleridge, another English poet, called this sense of time "cosmic consciousness."

When I came down from the hill, I happened to see a local fair had been organized, and I walked over. I spoke with a man selling guitars and told him my experience at the top. H asked if I wrote poetry. And he said he sometimes climbed to the top and sat under the same old tree to write lyrics for his songs. He then gave me a new term, "thin place," which he said was a way of describing the kind of experience I just had. A thin place, he said, is a place where the veil between the here and now and something beyond was lifted, if only for a minute or two, to enable one to see beyond the present moment into something just as real but deeper.

Since that experience in Wales, I have a new way of looking at life, staying awake to those moments that seem to break into time with new insights. It takes patience and wakefulness to be present when the veil separates between time in the here-and-now and some other reality to which we seldom pay attention. But I know these moments happen.

22. Have a Heart

I'VE ALWAYS CONSIDERED *The Wizard of Oz* to be one of the great sources of human wisdom.

It was one of the first movies I saw in a theater, during which I ran out crying after the wicked witch appeared. My sister had to entice me back in. but only after we sat in the back row and she bought me candy.

I've seen the movie so many more times, I always manage to see something new, which I believe is the sign of its importance.

The characters in the story illustrate some of the most important qualities of living well. The lion represents our need to be courageous, the tin man to think clearly, the scarecrow to feel deeply, and Dorothy to be at home.

The Grand Wizard of Oz may seem bungling, but he is wise. He knows that each of the other characters already possesses what they most want and simply needs someone to call attention to this. To each, he gives a symbol of their newfound gift—the tin man a heart, the lion a badge of courage, and the scarecrow a degree, a "doctor of thinkology."

Because he can't give Dorothy any tangible gift, he offers to take her home himself in the balloon in which he originally arrived. Of course, he inadvertently leaves without her, and she has to learn the lesson that all she has to do is tap her shoes and wish herself home.

Lately, I've felt the need for the tin man's gift of a heart that feels empathy for others. We've suffered too much hardheartedness and harsh words, denying the losses and burying the grief. We've had little tender-heartedness toward our losses, which, of course, is how we face grief together and find ways to deal with it.

As with individuals so, too, with nations—those who cannot grieve together, cannot heal together. That's why recently the simple act of lighting candles, a moment of silence, and hearing the sounds of "Amazing Grace" playing in front of the White House were so important. It gave us a chance to feel the losses of others and find sympathy for them.

23. Make Wise Decisions

WHEN I MENTION THE word "philosophy," what do you think about? Probably something heady, abstract, impractical. In one way, it can be all of these descriptions, but also much more.

Philosophy comes from the Greek, meaning the love of wisdom. But, then, what's wisdom? I think wisdom is learning how best to live. That's a practi cal, often personal, and sometimes important study.

Most of us think we know how best to live, but if we're honest don't really take much time to consider how to live a meaningful life. We succumb often to behaviors that don't help us or any others. There's a stimulus and our response. That's the basic description of human behavior.

But what if there could be a way to live more deeply, one over which we may have some control? What if we learned to pause taking any immediate response to stimuli outside our control and ask ourselves two questions that could change not only our immediate response but long-term implications, bringing us closer to who and what we want to be?

Here are two questions to ask before you make any big personal decision: First, how would you feel if someone did that to you? Second, what if everyone did what you propose to do?

If you take the time to ask these questions, that could change your future. But many do not have the time and are literally thrown into making a quick decision, one that might impact their lives for years to come?

Everyday Wisdom

One trick is simply paying attention to how you feel when pressed for an immediate response to a demand upon your life. If you can, take a time out and say you need to think about what you are being asked to do. Then ask the two questions before deciding.

Unfortunately, many are forced into life situations they did not really choose and often are not aware or strong enough to retreat or defer a decision. The decisions made under such circumstances may not be the best for the person. However, later if given time and patience the person involved may seek to understand the dynamics of the decision and make a decision about what was learned and not desired to be repeated. That's called learning.

Learning to fulfill one's purpose in life is one of the most fundamental issues anyone deals with. It's not always easily discerned. Sometimes it takes trials and errors to find the way right for you. Other times, the path is never found, and people wander through life wondering what it's all about.

For philosophy students I often give a simple exercise to begin thinking about their life vocation. On a piece of paper, I ask them not to think too much about the answer but let whatever comes, come. Here's the sentence I ask them to complete about themselves: I am here to: _____. I encourage them to write down their answers without thinking too much, but to trust what comes first.

It usually amazes me how often students worried about the question but never taken the time to write down their responses, and how often the responses are clear and given clues about how best to live.

I once had a student pull the same life examination trick on me. She asked me to write down my answer without thinking too much about it. Worse, she said I should write my response on the blackboard so everyone could see it.

This is what I wrote: "I am here to help myself and other people figure out why they are here."

Those words were my life mission, encapsulated in one sentence. I hadn't always followed that life mission. Sometimes I wandered along a different path, but in the long run I realized this

23. Make Wise Decisions

expressed who I knew myself to be and what I hoped to be and do for others.

Try the experiment. On a sheet of paper complete the sentence in terms of your life: I am here to _____. And then take a quiet minute to think about your life, past, present, and hopes for the future. This is called wisdom.

24. Practice Being Kind

THERE SEEM TO BE so many ways to think about what is right and wrong. I believe that sometimes people use this variety of opinions as an excuse for not taking anything seriously. They assume tolerance implies accepting every statement as equally valid, which would mean that you can't complain about intolerance either since there are no standards.

Are there any time-tested ethical principles or rules that seem to emerge in various cultures? I've heard this question asked many times when someone confronts an ethical issue. Often, people answer, "It's all relative," which I believe means that they aren't sure if there are any hard and fast rules that apply to every situation. There's some truth in that statement, but we tend to get so arrogant that we believe only our opinion is the true one. Respecting differences is an important way to live and grow and I hope part of what it means to be an educated person. But having an opinion is also important, as long as you are open to testing and changing it when required.

Without some central moral focus, we cannot judge others no matter what they do.

While there may be no absolutely perfect moral rule, there is one that history seems to believe is crucial for a moral life, whether that of an individual or of society. It's called the Golden Rule, and I have found upwards of fifteen different versions of this rule in many cultures and times. This rule usually is expressed as treating others as you wish to be treated.

24. Practice Being Kind

One word that helps to make the Golden Rule clear is compassion. Compassion means not only showing kindness to ourselves but to others, a deep feeling of sympathy toward them and a commitment to helping alleviate their suffering. Compassion is active, not passive. It's what I would call "practical philosophy" of a way of life that sits at the heart of many spiritual traditions.

And here's the most important lesson I learned from my teachers: what one believes and how one lives are not opposites, but complementary qualities. Sometimes how you live speaks as clearly as what you say you believe. These two faculty members taught compassion but also were compassionate. They took time with me. They listened to me. Those are the keys to healthy relationships with oneself, others and indeed, the whole world. And they are the keys, I believe, to learning how to be a whole person in a broken world.

25. Turn Off, Tune In, Drop In

"Turn on, tune in, drop out."

These were the words of advice of Timothy Leary in the Sixties at a gathering of mostly young people at the Golden Gate Park in San Francisco. It was a generation of drugs, protests, recreational sex, and opposition to authority figures.

I survived the Sixties and did not take Leary's advice. I stayed involved in the world around me then, and still try to do the same today.

But if I were to come up with a catch phrase for what I see happening today, it would be: "Turn off, tune in, drop in."

Simply put, here is what I mean;

"Turn off." Because of the informational explosion from which we seem unable to escape, we have learned how to engage in multiple tasks at the same time while also paying no attention to any of the data presented. We have been conditioned to think quickly but not deeply. We need to be very selective in what information we receive and from where.

"Tune in." In the Sixties the world could not be avoided. There were riots in the streets, a war raging and a draft, plus a president who created enemy lists and ways to get information illegally about his political opponents. Tune into quieter, more gentle activities which soothe your soul, not assault your intelligence.

"Drop in." Find a group or organization whose values you hold and get involved. Pick one or two to avoid burnout.

25. Turn Off, Tune In, Drop In

A few months ago, while giving students a break midway through a class, I wandered into the hallway outside and saw two standing a few feet apart, tapping text messages on their cell phones. When I asked what they were doing, they said they were communicating with one another. When I remarked that they could talk to one another in person, one responded as if I were an alien from a different planet: "That's just not the way we communicate these days."

I fear we are witnessing a generation that can do many things at the same time, but not do one important thing for a long time. We have learned how to give and take information from many sources, but not know how to detect what is important from what is trivia.

Here are few words of advice:

Turn off the daily information blasts coming at you from every direction. Take a walk. Use five minutes each day to sit quietly. Pause and practice reading a few sentences in books that have been passed down from generation to generation to offer wisdom.

Tune in to the voice within you that the ancients called your conscience or soul and listen to what it says. It may take a while to dismiss the informational clutter stored within yourself. I

Drop in to programs or organizations that need your help. There are many, from those delivering meals on wheels to others mentoring students in schools. In the midst of cruelty and chaos, perhaps engaging in simple acts of helping others may yet bring us to what Abraham Lincoln in his first inaugural address called "the better angels of our nature."

26. Say and Act What You Believe

THERE ARE NO MORE disrupting words than these two: cognitive dissonance. Most of us may never have heard them, but they result in much upheaval and suffering in life.

What is cognitive dissonance? Here's one definition: the state of having inconsistent thoughts, beliefs, or attitudes, especially as relating to behavioral decisions and attitude change.

You can spot cognitive dissonance by simply observing people who say one thing but act differently. When asked to name the kinds of people who do so may respond by saying politicians or salespersons or sometimes clergy.

Nothing drives people away from institutions quicker than cognitive dissonance, when members claim one thing but act quite differently. This is certainly true for religious institutions where certain values or beliefs are expressed but not lived.

I remember one congregation which professed itself to be loving but which was fighting over who was in power or which beliefs were not acceptable. Only people of a certain spiritual or political or racial characteristic were welcome. This belief kept some in power but the out crowd out. This belief was enforced not directly but indirectly by comments about certain religious or political views as unacceptable.

Newcomers especially pick up the climate of any community simply through observation. They note who is acceptable or not and whether the institution practices what it preaches. That's why it's important for any institution to seek the opinions

26. Say and Act What You Believe

of those outside, since those inside had become so accustomed to behaviors, they could not see them. I remember when I used to do consulting work with a congregation facing some growth issues that resulted in limited budgets. I noted during a worship service that no offering was collected but a plate left at the back of the sanctuary, hidden to one side. When I asked a leader why, he said that was just the way things were. He made no connection to the group's dwindling funds.

The chief way to break through cognitive dissonance is truth telling. It's not easy because insiders are the ones who determine what truth is and don't usually appreciate anyone with different points of view. But you will learn little without consciously seeking points of view different from your own.

27. Shape, Don't Fear, the Unknown

FEAR IS THE POWER that immobilizes action.

It is the same reality which faces us today, fearing the unknown we cling to fake news from many sources, leaders who react emotionally rather than rationally, terror which tells us to expect the worst without dealing creatively with the present.

There is a great deal to scare us these days if we focus only on fear of the unknown. We do not know what will happen when two countries yell threats at one another, or when one country seeks to influence the elections of others, or when the gulf between the wealthy and the poor increases across the world. We become paralyzed, thinking problems so vast no one can solve them. It doesn't help when we join the chorus of naysayers who want to tear down our constitution, degrade our institutions, and tell us they are our only hope.

The unknown is not determined in advance. It is shaped by what we do today. There is not some force of history or nature that is chiseled in stone, never to be changed. Why fear the unknown but the unknown is not here? We are incapacitated by fear itself, and it is often sown by those who wish to keep us in the control. They feed off fear to stay in power.

If the unknown had shaped early American history, driving people to accept their fears, there would have been no American republic. And there may be no vibrant republic if we give into our fears and turn over our power to change the future to those who would change it to benefit themselves.

27. Shape, Don't Fear, the Unknown

What kind of a country might result if we say no to the naysayers and yes to those who paint a different vision of who we might become, a nation where people are judged on the content of their character and not the color of their skin, where every person has an opportunity to fulfill a dream, where we seek to sow peace not war in the world, where our leaders represent the best of our creed, that every person has the right to" life, liberty and the pursuit of happiness?"

We are either going to be inspired by a dream or drawn into chaos by fear. Which path we take will shape who we become. The choice is yours.

28. Think before Acting

METAPHYSICAL ETHICS IS THAT branch of philosophy which deals with the big questions of life, the ones that puzzle and sometimes confound us, but which from time to time bother us, usually in times of crisis, whether personal or societal. Some of these questions include: Why is there something at all? Why do bad things happen to good people? Why do good things happen to bad people? Is there a purpose not only to our lives but to the universe as a whole? And the one most frequently asked: Does everything happen for a reason (or a purpose)?

Why there may be no definitive answer to the question of why things happen, whether they have purpose that will satisfy every person, everyone at some point in their lives faces such a question and arrives at some response that at least satisfies them. The question is deeply personal, one that only you can respond to out of your life. So, take a moment to reflect on your life now.

Think of a time in your life when you faced a crisis. one that possibly at the time it happened you saw no way through. Now look back and think what happened. Was there a purpose served in the long run? Now, think in a wider framework of a historical event when the life of the world faced a crisis Think of what happened. Was there a purpose?

One might suggest there are two main ways to respond to the question of whether or not things happen for a reason or purpose. One might argue that natural events happen for a reason, the cause-and-effect principle—that there are certain universal

28. Think before Acting

laws such as gravity that apply at all times and places. But when it comes to purpose, things don't often follow reason. Some events which impact us do not seem to have a purpose. A tornado hits and seems to take life indiscriminately.

On the other hand, others say that life generally as a purpose, either individually or the universe.

Here are two questions to think about:

1. In terms of your own life, do things seem to happen for a purpose?
2. In terms of the universe, do things seem to happen for a purpose?

29. Think of the Ends and Means

Here's a word that some feel old fashioned but one I feel is desperately needed in the political climate in which we now live: honor.

What does it mean to be a person of honor? It means someone who is recognized not only for what they achieve but who they are—their character in other words.

Fortunately, there are still persons of honor who put public service above private gain, who try to live ethically by adhering to certain principles such as fairness and integrity, and who strive for the common good rather than selfish outcomes.

Unfortunately, there are others who put their own gains above the public good, whose principles are secondary to winning at any cost, and who attack those with whom they have disagreements.

There's another often-unused word that describes honorable people: Character. A person of character is someone of moral excellence, someone we hold up to help guide us.

Here's another description you don't spoken often enough when it comes to who we honor: role model. A role model is someone we identify as worthy of being followed.

I know there are some persons alive today who are role models, but I am interested in citing two from the past who are often used to guide us today: Marcus Aurelius, emperor of the Roman Empire during its Golden Age, and George Washington, first president of the United States in its earliest years of the republic. Both men were both political and military leaders.

29. Think of the Ends and Means

Aurelius, who died in 121, was also a philosopher. His book of meditations is still cited today for its guidance on how best to live. If you want to read a book about how best to be an ethical leader, reading his meditations is a great place to begin.

30. Be a Hero

WHEN I WAS A young boy growing up in Philadelphia, I was sent to spend a summer with my brother. He lived in a rural area that had one small town surrounded by farms and scattered houses. I suppose my parents felt it would be good for me to escape the noise and congestion of city life.

Growing up in Philadelphia where sports is really a religion, I gravitated to playing in a church softball league. The teams were chosen by location, the town teams versus those in more rural areas. But when one rural team did not have a full roster, I was chosen for that team.

My team consisted of players from one of the poorest areas where most men worked in a tannery or on a farm, and where a one-room schoolhouse served most of the children. It was a strange world for me, this city slicker. The team uniforms were put together by parents, the gloves stitched as well. Later, I would proudly call my team the Tannery Nine. Because I was smaller, I played second base, where the manager thought I probably would cause the least damage. I also batted eighth for the same reason. In this way, I stayed in the background as best I could and considered myself fortunate to catch or hit a ball.

The season came down to a final game, the Tannery Nine facing the town team with its new uniforms and gloves. We were winning five to four in the bottom of the last inning. I had done little to help, fielding one ground ball, striking out twice and hitting a weak grounder to third base.

30. Be a Hero

There were two outs, the town team had the bases loaded. The final hitter, one who had previously hit a ball over the leftfield wall, was up. He hit the ball right at me. Time froze. Without thinking, I jumped as high as I could, stuck my glove up in the air, and felt the ball sting my hand. The ball started to roll out, but I held on. What happened next is still a blur. All I remember is being at the bottom of a pile of my teammates, a hero.

Of all the things I have done in my life, I still consider this one of my greatest moments, I think because I overcame great odds.

Here's the good news: every person has a moment of greatness in them. For me it was softball game playing for the Tannery Nine. Look deep within and you will find your Kairos moment. Remember and rejoice.

31. Tend a Garden

IN ONE OF THE most remarkably out-of-character statements ever made in literature, sleuth and rationalist Sherlock Holmes said, almost whimsically, "Flowers are nature's surest sign of Providence."

I am not sure what case he was handling at the time or whether by some stroke of fortune, he simply had a moment to smell the roses in an English country garden, but I do know that gardens are like outdoor altars where you can sit quietly and soak life throwing off its winter garments and poking its head through the thawing earth.

I come from a long line of Welsh and English gardeners. Though I grew up in Philadelphia, I can still remember the garden outside our back window and the return of the same turtle every year to a batch of high grass near the drain pipe. Even then, concrete walls and traffic notwithstanding, spring came as a joyful surprise every year, reminding me that all life seeks to move toward the light, if given half a chance.

There are some places this year where I imagine spring will come slowly: in foreign lands torn by wars or in some of our own neighborhoods where dreams die. Raised a Calvinist I expect the worst, but am growing to see hope rise every spring with the first sign of daffodils or the sound of a bat cracking from the nearby sandlot.

You can learn a great deal by sitting near a garden. If nothing else, you will be able to refrain from causing other people more problems.

31. Tend a Garden

There is something humbling about planting a garden, especially for a city slicker like me. You toss a few bulbs in before winter and, presto, without so much as lifting a shovel or rake, the green shoots come bursting out of the earth, which had been so barren and cold for so long. Talk about the simple graces of life—nothing equals the sight of yellow and blue and red and orange sending their flares into the sunlight.

I also understand more why diversity is beautiful from studying my garden. The blue flowers do not say to the red, "Get out of here, this is our spot of the earth!" The orange does not seize the green buds by the stems and try to toss them out of their space. The beauty of a garden is that each flower retains its uniqueness, but when joined together with others forms a patchwork tapestry of joy. Stand back a few feet when your garden is in full bloom and observe its majesty, just as marvelous as seeing the blue planet earth from the distance of the moon.

There is an old proverb: "Many things grow in the garden that were never sowed there." That's the really humbling part of growing a life or a garden. No matter how carefully you plant the seeds, a few weeds always manage to grow. You can't control them any more than you can control the people around you. And, sometimes, even weeds add a touch of diversity to a flower patch or a crack in the city sidewalk.

Amid the sounds of bombs and planes and conflicts, a garden, like poetry, draws us inward to some magical place we thought lost in childhood. And the news is good: Life renews itself. To that, we can all say, "Amen."

32. Use Common Sense

COMMON SENSE IS NOT so common. Nor is it often based on what our senses tell us to be true.

Our senses may sometimes deceive us, but they remain our best guides to knowing who we are and what kind of world we inhabit.

When someone says, "Let me be perfectly clear," they are about listen skeptically as they twist and distract. That's the main reason in our time truth is hard to find—the motives are disguised and hidden from view, so that after a while you give up thinking there is any truth at all. It's all fake news or someone trying to sell you something, whether a product or a candidate.

Without guidelines for trying to figure out what is true from what is not, we cannot figure out what to decide. It's the issue of our time really—sometimes disguised under words like toleration where everything goes and only truth leaves. Some ethicists say that relativity is the problem, where we excuse anything because we don't want to be labeled "intolerant."

I believe that some things are truer than others, that there are some things we should not tolerate.

I am not willing to tolerate people lying and calling it truth. For example, global warming is real, not a fiction. You can disagree about how much is caused by humans or by natural cycles. But it is a reality and those who deny it are bringing harm to all of us.

I believe in using our brains to find common ground, accepting where we differ but also where we find ourselves in agreement.

32. Use Common Sense

So much time and negative energy go into pointing out differences that we sometimes forget we share a common humanity.

I believe that kindness and generosity and compassion are at the heart of what the world's great spiritual traditions, often cited by not always lived, by individuals or groups. It's important what you believe, but how you live speaks volumes about who you really are.

33. Become a Role Model

Here's a word that some feel old fashioned but one I feel is desperately needed in the political climate in which we now live: honor.

What does it mean to be a person of honor? It means someone who is recognized not only for what they achieve but who they are—their character, in other words.

Fortunately, there are still people of honor who put public service above private gain, who try to live ethically by adhering to certain principles such as fairness and integrity, and who strive for the common good rather than selfish outcomes.

Unfortunately, there are others who put their own gains above the public good, whose principles are secondary to winning at any cost, and who attack those with whom they have disagreements.

There's another often-unused word that describes honorable people: Character. A person of character is someone of moral excellence, someone we hold up to help guide us.

Here's another description you don't spoken often enough when it comes to who we honor: role model. A role model is someone we identify as worthy of being followed.

I know there are some people alive today who are role models, but I am interested in citing two from the past who are often used to guide us today: Marcus Aurelius, emperor of the Roman Empire during its Golden Age, and George Washington, president of the United States in its earliest years of the republic. Both men were both political and military leaders.

33. Become a Role Model

Aurelius, who died in 121, was also a philosopher. His book of meditations is still cited today for its guidance on how best to live. If you want to read a book about how best to be an ethical leader, reading his meditations is a great place to begin.

34. Assume the Middle Way

ASSUMING A MODERATE POSITION these days gets bad or sometimes no press at all.

Moderation in all things is ancient and usually good advice, not often heeded in the age in which we live where extreme views grab the headlines or cyberspace. No wonder we feel worried about the state of things.

Go ahead and call me names, but I want to assert that the moderate or middle ground is where truth can be found.

But in most cases moderation is the best position, and it comes with a great philosophical pedigree.

More than 2,500 years ago the Greek philosopher Aristotle spoke of what he called the Golden Mean. The basic principle was to seek balance or the middle way between extremes of excess and deficiency. Neither too much nor too little might be simplest way to state his case.

For example, take the virtue of courage. One extreme would be fool heartedness, the deficiency would be cowardice. The art of living would be to gravitate toward the middle, neither making foolish decisions or no decisions at all. Aristotle argued that as rational creatures choosing the middle path would lead to a better life.

Today, at least in our political life, we seem to disavow moderation, going to one extreme or the other, left or right. No wonder our policy discussions are so fraught with conflicts. We can't reach any consensus because we seldom seek the middle ground, and those who do are criticized.

34. Assume the Middle Way

I'd like to argue that sometimes finding consensus or the middle ground may be the best path toward progress.

Take the issue of voting which seems to separate us into camps. One camp wants to secure voting even if that means restricting it while the other to expand and increase it. One says the last presidential election was stolen, the other that no one has shown any wide voter fraud which would have changed the outcome.

Perhaps, using the middle way model, we can find common ground. What might the middle way be? Perhaps to make voting accessible to as many people as want to vote, while at the same time making sure votes are accurately tallied by impartial counters.

Most of us, I suspect, are not in the extreme left or right, although that's where we appear to be when you listen to or watch the media. We become what we hear or watch, thus feeding the frenzy.

Most of us are somewhere in the middle when it comes to our views. We may be left or right center, but it's still the center. We want to find common ground. It's seeking and acting on that consensus that may yield the results most of desire—common sense solutions.

It's hard to find the middle way when people are screaming or turning fellow citizens into enemies. The democratic process may be messy. No one may get everything they want. But finding common ground is essential. Without that we may end divided, frustrated, and less than we might have become.

35. Practice Dying

MORE OFTEN THAN NOT difficult thoughts come at times when we face death, a reality most of us seldom talk about but all must face. I have found such times to be full of meaning we miss going about our daily lives.

The other day "Grandma" died. She was a thirteen-year-old feral cat living near our back yard. My wife faithfully cared for her as if she were one of the other three felines who lived in our home with a rescued beagle, Annie, who had been found wandering pregnant in the Tennessee woods. We are a household of misfits, myself one of them.

The dying cat was rescued by one neighbor, then another to wrap her in a blanket and later help bury her in our backyard. They were good neighbors, ones you seldom hear about but give you reason to hope in a sometimes-cruel world.

When you love anything, you must also learn to let go. Those who love most, often hurt most when facing loss. Perhaps that's why Plato when asked to summarize his philosophy reportedly said: "Practice dying." He meant that by learning to accept losses as part of life, we learn to live deeper lives.

In a world filled with seemingly epic events—wars and rumors of wars, pandemics and stock market losses, it's hopeful to remember those little, nameless acts of kindness and love. In truth, these acts may express the essence of what philosophy and religion have been pointing us toward all along, the real reason we are here at all—to help one another, the essence of the Golden Rule.

35. Practice Dying

Many years and neighbors ago, another spotted me feeding the sparrows outside and spoke to me because she cared for another creature who came each morning to feed upon her back porch. I ended reflecting on her wisdom silently at first but eventually took form in a poem with these words:

"I know I cannot save all these tiny birds.
But I can scatter seed in hope one or two survive.
And if I make light the burdens of their beating hearts,
in heaven's eye that might be enough"

There is a moral gulf so great we cannot fantom it between those who save lives and those who take them, between those who hate others and those who love them, between those who cause pain and those who ease the pains of others.

I choose to honor those who nurture life, not those who abuse it. They are the beacons of hope in a cold and sometimes dangerous world.

36. Temporarily Suspend Doubt

I GREW UP IN a Philadelphia minister's family. I could not escape any holiday season because I grew up in a parsonage connected to the sanctuary. I was trapped.

When you grow up literally immersed in church life, you learn that what people say they believe and how they sometimes act are not the same. I became naturally skeptical of the temporary glow of the Christmas season, knowing that soon after December 25 people would return to their typically bah humbug behaviors.

I was a determined skeptic. My child's resolve was to prove Santa a fake.

It started when my mother took me to see Santa at a downtown department store. As I sat on his lap, I pulled on his white beard hoping to reveal he was fake news. The problem was that it was a real beard and all Santa could do was say ouch and a low "ho, ho, ho" and push me away.

But I was not defeated in unmasking this elf.

It was the family custom on Christmas eve for Santa to come to the parsonage door and leave presents behind. After a few years, I became convinced that Santa was really my father, his laughter slightly British, like my father.

I planned ahead. One Christmas I asked for a fingerprint kit, so I could dust the fire place and get fingerprints. I was a curious, devious kid and waited an entire year to use the kit on the next Christmas eve. On Christmas morning, I rushed downstairs to examine any prints but there were none. My father lurked nearby

36. Temporarily Suspend Doubt

and smiled. "That elf is a smart old man," he said laughing. "You can't trip him up that easily."

I had to wait another year. This time I grew more devious. I waited for Santa to come to our door on Christmas eve. I wanted to out my father as the jolly elf. When Santa arrived at the front door I called upstairs to my father, who each year claimed to be in his office working on a sermon. I knew I had him. Even he couldn't be in two places at the same time.

From the testimony of eyewitnesses (my mother and a sister) when my father came downstairs, my eyes grew larger, and I turned my head back and forth to see him and the Santa at my front door, who by now was really bellowing out his "ho, ho, ho," and handing me a bag of candy. I was stunned into silence and soon questioning my own skepticism.

I had a few more good years when I didn't pull at Santa's beard. I suspended my doubts and just enjoyed the warmth of the season, the gift giving and singing and the sounds and smells of Christmas. There would be time enough later to doubt.

The philosopher Aristotle said that philosophy begins in wonder. I would add it sometimes ends in doubt. But what I learned as a child still helps me realize today that not every truth is able to be proven scientifically, that sometimes truth is about the lure of stories and fables and myths that take us into imaginative realms where reason refuses to go.

(*Oh, reader alert: the "Santa" at the door was a neighbor my father had arranged to take his place*).

37. Don't Waste Time

BUT WHAT IS TIME?

It would seem obvious measuring time is easy. Check your watch or cell phone and they tell you. That is time measured by quantity, how many minutes and hours have been counted. But it's only the right time and year if you accept one calendar over another.

But is time the same for everyone? Or is it relevant to our perceptions of it? Consider how time is measured by someone enjoying conversation with a friend against waiting for an egg to boil. Or, better, place your hand on a hot stove and see how long a few seconds feel/

There are two Greek words for time that help to unlock its meaning. Chronos is clock time, measured by the commonly accepted standards. It's what we mean when we share the time of day. It's time by its quantity or numbers.

But there's another Greek word for time that unlocks a different, more nuanced understand. It's Kairos time, which is measured by its quality, its depth, not its length. This is a different way of measuring time, and one that yields wisdom for how best to live.

Every human life has elements of both quantity and quality times. It's easier to measure quantity. Someone can say they are thirty years old. That's Chronos, pure and simple. But what I ask you to measure Kairos time? How would you respond?

37. Don't Waste Time

One way to describe Kairos time in your life is to ask when were the decisive moments in your life when something very important happened, when you were aware of a great moment or change.

Looking for Kairos moments in your life are great ways to understand yourself, what really matters to you. The great moments of your life may at first seem obvious—when you made a decision about your vocation or partner or moving to a new area. But sometimes what may seem unimportant at the moment assume life changing when you look back.

The trick to finding Kairos in your life is staying awake to when it happens. You will feel its impact when it happens, and only looking back realize its ripple effect. Looking back, I realize my Kairos time was when a fourth-grade teacher took pity on me after I started public school after early years in a more experimental learning environment. She saw my struggle but also my writing abilities, and encouraged me not only to write but to share my stories with the class. At the time it didn't seem like much, but as I look back it was that moment, I realized what I was called to be and do in life in whatever form that has taken, from writing books and columns to teaching. In ancient times it might be said my fate was shaped.

As I have grown older and a little wiser, I have learned that how you spend time shapes the contours of your life. If you waste or misuse it you may never fulfill your purpose. If you pay attention to when Kairos happens and learn from it, you will find who you are and your purpose.

38. Find Your Story

THE MESSAGE ON THE shirt worn by the grocery store clerk caught my eye: "Life is a journey."

Normally I am hit with so many messages from so many sources during any day that I tuned them out just as I do candidates thirty-second pitches for being elected. They drone on, I tune out.

But this clerk's message haunted me. I think now I know why.

Life is a journey. This sentence is a great metaphor for unlocking not only one's own life but that of others.

Life is a journey from birth to death and perhaps beyond. The journey is filled with stories, not only our own but those we love and, of course, the great universal stories of humankind.

What makes and keeps us human beings? The stories we tell and share with others, sometimes drawn by our ancient ancestors on the walls of caves or told around campfires or even shared online.

We are the storytellers. We are here to share ours and listen to others.

My brother died not long ago. He was a storyteller as a teacher, writer, and preacher. We shared our own stories over many years, achievements and failures. Our stories changed over the years of sharing them, but the spirit in which they were given remained—the stories were told as they really happened, although as good storytellers they might be sometimes embellished. But the stories

38. Find Your Story

were heard. After all, listening is a rare art these days. And hearing is the process by which wisdom is gained.

I remember the story told by my sister, another teacher in the family.

There was a teacher getting ready to retire. He had spent a lifetime teaching in a small village in another country. He collected seashells as a hobby. His students wanted to give him a gift so they walked many miles over rough terrain to get to the coast where they gathered shells. At this retirement party, the students presented the shells to him. He said how grateful he was for the gift. One student replied: "No, teacher, shells were not the gift. The gift was the journey."

In a very simple but profound way the stories we make and share are the heart of our journeys. Some stories are full of joy, some of sadness. Some are hopeful, some not. Some stories are kept private, others shared freely. If we live well, no story is ever wasted in the grand scheme of things.

Ask yourself what kind of story you are in. My brother spent a lifetime writing and leading groups about telling their stories. His book about this is still available on Amazon-Richard L. Morgan, "Remembering Your Story."

Over the many years of our conversations, we spoke often with one another, not just about everyday things but of life's meaning, which in the past few years touched on a theme which is seldom spoken honestly but is the heart of philosophy: death. It's a topic we avoid because it is often out of our control. But facing death makes every moment of living deeper. As my brother wrote in a book about his work with dementia patients, "no act of love is ever wasted."

39. Stay Curious

WHEN SOME THEOLOGIANS LONG ago claimed the earth was the center of the universe, thus falsely claiming we humans were at the heart of everything, one scientist, Galileo, using a telescope revealed a much better understanding of the universe, that we were one of many planets circling around the sun.

When others asked the question of what was out there, explorers from England and Spain sailed the sea to find civilizations, some older than the ones they left in Europe.

And when some asked what was out there in the deep regions of space, others planned and sometimes carried out journeys to the moon or mars or took photos of new planets never before seen.

Not knowing is the source of new knowledge, the basis of all new scientific understandings which, in turn, will be questioned and lead to new knowledge. Not knowing is the mark of a curious person who wants to know more. Not wanting to know more is the mark of a self-satisfied, smug person who thinks he or she is the end of all human knowledge.

In the modern age, besides wanting to know what's out there, some want to understand better responses to a different question: "What's in here?" By "here," they mean inside us, especially how our minds work (or don't).

It's an old argument about whether the mind is part of the brain, and thus material, or part of some immaterial reality called consciousness. It's another version of what came first, the chicken

39. Stay Curious

or the egg. That's why it seems to be mind-body ought to be hyphenated since they exist in relationship to one another.

Know-it-alls really don't know much, while those who remain open to new truths are often wiser.

40. Ten Suggestions for Living Well

SOME PEOPLE THINK YOU must go to college to study ethics. But all you need do is take the time to think about your life. It was Socrates, considered to be one of the earliest philosophers, who provided one of the earliest and most used definitions of ethics: it is about how best to live.

You can learn ethics by staying awake, learning from your life and perhaps consulting with the thoughts of some of the world's great ethicists in their writings. Of course, Socrates didn't write anything, but his thoughts were written down by his pupil, Plato.

In ancient times ethics was conceived as commandments, hence the Ten Commandments. It seems that many books these days are written with lists of ten items, such as Ten Ways to Find Your Job (or mate). So, let me add to the growing list of books with ten suggestions with my version of Ten Principles for Living Well, which I learned from my own life and a few wise friends.

Ten Principles of Living Well:

1. Know yourself, your strengths and weaknesses.

2. Don't do anything today you will regret tomorrow.

3. Don't blame others for your own mistakes.

4. Do unto others as you would have them do unto you.

5. Be compassionate.

6. Take time to play.

7. Learn how to listen to yourself and others.

40. Ten Suggestions for Living Well

8. Understand what can be changed and what cannot.
9. Find and live your purpose for being here.
10. Treat your body and spirit wisely.

And the eleventh principle to keep you humble and sane: Forgive yourself for violating one or more of the suggestions every day, because no one is perfect. In fact, if you try to be perfect in everything you probably won't succeed at much.

Living well has something to do with a quality we seem to have forgotten these days: Character. Character is who and what you are within. It's what you do when you don't think anyone is watching. Character is formed through habits, what you do or don't do regularly. Obviously, there are good and bad habits, good or bad character.

It used to be that good character was thought to be the result of good parenting. Many of the values we think to be important, such as honesty and trustworthiness, were learned first at home.

Developing good character also used to be considered part of education. We wanted students to be honest and fair, get along with others, tell the truth, and not cheat. And for centuries, we believed character was best explained in our religious institutions or spiritual traditions.

Whenever I want to think about a person's character, I ask myself a simple question: Would I want my child to grow up to be such a person? This question clarifies what anyone really feels is most important about living.

Of course, no one is perfect; everyone has strengths and weaknesses. The trick is learning how to build on strengths and learn from weaknesses. But over the years I have come to respect people who have made decisions that benefit themselves and others in rough times. Aristotle called this ability phronesis or practical wisdom. It is the highest form of ethical behavior, the mark of a wise person who having made a mistake tries not to repeat it, but lead a better life.

Exercises for Self-Reflection

Create Your Book of Life

Everyone has a book of life, a series of stories to tell. A book of life has a title, chapters (roughly seven years equals one chapter), and episodes in each chapter. Every book of life is unique, although there are often common themes that cut across time and cultures. In the spaces below, give your book of life a title, then a title to each chapter (e.g., chapter 1 equals the first seven years of your life), then make notes about important events or people that you think are important in that particular chapter. If you want to understand more about yourself, find someone you trust to tell your story using this guide or, better yet, have them complete the same exercise, then each one shares their story.

YOUR BOOK OF LIFE TITLE:

_____

Chapter 1 _____ (age 0–7)

    Notes on events or people:

Chapter 2 _____ (age 8–14)

Chapter 3 _____ (age 15–21)

Chapter 4 _____ (age 22–29)

Chapter 5 _____ (age 30–37)

Exercises for Self-Reflection

Chapter 6 _____ (age 38–45)

Chapter 7 _____ (age 46–53)

Chapter 8 _____ (age 54–61)

Chapter 9 _____ (age 62–69)

Chapter 10 _____ (age 70–77)

Chapter 11 _____ (age 78–85)

Chapter 12 _____ (age 86–93)

Chapter 13 _____ (age 94–101)

Chapter 14 _____ (age 101 and over)

Keep a Journal

A journal is one of the best ways to take a look at your journey through life. A journal can be personal and private, usually in book form, or more public, like a blog

First, you need to purchase a journal. You can find them for as little as a dollar or more if you want fancy ones that can be locked. Check out local bookstores or Amazon.com.

Second, you need to say to yourself that this journal is really yours for one simple reason—you can write honestly and read it later knowing it expresses your innermost thoughts and feelings.

If you use a blog for your journal, remember it is public and not just for your eyes.

Third, you need to commit yourself to maintain the journal at least for the length of a month or longer, writing in it every day, even if a few words or sentences, a drawing or scribble.

Fourth, the journal is "Reflections on My Life," which means just that—whatever you think is important in your life is "grist for the mill" and can be written about in the journal.

It is also a reflective journal, which means you are being asked not only what happened to you, but also what meaning you make of it.

Exercises for Self-Reflection

Fifth, use a pen to write in the journal (handwriting is an extension of ourselves and often a way to slow ourselves down long enough to write).

How you organize your journal is up to you. Here is how I organize mine.

I list the date at the top of a page.

Each morning I begin with a few moments of silence or a few simple readings. I think about the day ahead. If anything strikes me as important, I jot down a few notes in the journal.

Some evenings I take a few minutes to think about the day, and jot down a few notes to remind myself of what happened and what it might mean.

At the end of a week, I look over my notes for that week and jot down any concluding reflections of what happened and what it means.

Sample Entry

Ran into a neighbor I hadn't seen for a while. He crossed the street to say hello. He and I had been part of a neighborhood group and gotten to know one another. We talked (mainly he) about the fact that he and his wife had been hospitalized for nearly six weeks and how difficult it had been. What dawned on me was how little people know one another in their own neighborhoods.

I hadn't even realized he hadn't been there. It also struck me how important the informal and regular ties are between people; sometimes it is easier to think about saving the world than paying attention to the needs of those who live nearby. And, finally, having been in a hospital for nearly two weeks and still recovering from the experiences, I realized how much I could have showed empathy and offer an understanding ear. How easy it is to express concern for those you don't know, but how difficult to care for those you do know.

Exercises for Self-Reflection

Conduct Your Annual Checkup

Call this an annual ethical checkup, or basic ethics. From time to time, I go back to what I believe to be the essentials of how I reach moral decisions. I do this as much for myself as others to establish some of the criteria I use.

First, ethics is most easily described as learning how best to live, as individuals and whole societies. It's about describing what's right or wrong, culturally if not universally, but also what good or bad in any given situation. It's an imprecise guide, but at least one that offers clues about morality, summarized the best we can from great ethical teachings.

When I evaluate ethical choices, it's usually in retrospect. That, looking back we can see the implications of choices made. I wish I could say I thought carefully about any decision before I make it (and try to do so), but many times I am literally thrown into situations without being given much time to make a choice.

There are two great ethical traditions that help me learn. The first is called Utilitarianism and its basis focus is to seek the greatest good for the greatest number of people. It's often used in making decisions about limited resources, making the choice that will positively impact the greatest number of people. The second moral tradition I consult from the great ethical teacher Immanuel Kant. He urged us to look at the intentions of any decision made, not only the results. It may be that a person's intentions were good but the results were not because there may be unintentional consequences.

Two of the world's greatest philosophers, Socrates and Aristotle, had some sage guidance about living a more ethical and better life.

Socrates said you need to know yourself. Actually, this Greek aphorism was one of the maxims inscribed in the Temple of Apollo at Delphi. The other two were "nothing to excess" and "certainty brings insanity."

Exercises for Self-Reflection

Aristotle wrote that the key to living a good life was adopting good habits. You grow by practicing good behavior and avoiding bad behavior.

I suspect many perceive philosophy to be quite removed from daily life, but ethics, sometimes called "practical philosophy" seeks to provide guidance on how best to live. It offers wisdom based on reason and experience for becoming all you are capable of becoming.

Knowing yourself is the key to make wiser choices. Most of us don't make wise decisions because we haven't taken time to reflect on who are we. We can only do this by using our reason to take stock of what we have learned by living. Reason and experience are the twin qualities that are basic to human beings, according to Socrates and Aristotle.

Self-knowledge is also the key to adopting habits that benefit your quality of life. In order to live a moral life, Aristotle would say, you must choose the values by which you wish to live and seek to avoid those that diminish yourself. For example, if you wish to be a compassionate person, you must practice being compassionate.

I've often thought that just as doctors and lawyers have practices, so, too, must every human being who wishes to live a virtuous life. It's called "character development," a term seldom used these days as much as it should be.

When we say a person is a great or good character, I think we know what that implies. He or she is virtuous, choosing positive virtues, such as courage and compassion, over negative ones, such as revenge and gluttony. It is a matter of personal choice how best (or worse) to live, practiced over a lifetime.

Of course, no one is perfect. Those who think they are, really aren't practicing being a good person. Everyone makes mistakes and fails. The trick is learning not to repeat them. Becoming a good person involves learning from mistakes and growing in self-knowledge over a lifetime.

About the Author

JOHN C. MORGAN HAS been a journalist, minister, agency director, and college professor. But he's always been a writer. He holds three graduate degrees in philosophy, ethics, and religious history. He lives with his wife, three cats, and one dog in Pennsylvania (where he was born). Resource Publications has published another of his books, *A Little Wisdom for Growing Up,* which might complement this book. It's a collection of fables and stories for children and adults to explore moral issues and life lessons.

www.ingramcontent.com/pod-product-compliance
Lightning Source LLC
Chambersburg PA
CBHW071155090426
42736CB00012B/2337